Culinary Travel Journal

The pleasure of eating is of all ages,
all conditions, all countries, and all days.

—ANTHELME BRILLAT-SAVARIN

CULINARY
TRAVEL JOURNAL

TEN SPEED PRESS
Berkeley • *Toronto*

Ten Speed Press
P.O. Box 7123
Berkeley, California 94707
www.tenspeed.com

A Kirsty Melville Book

Distributed in Australia by Simon and Schuster Australia, in Canada by Ten Speed Press Canada, in New Zealand by Southern Publishers Group, in South Africa by Real Books, in Southeast Asia by Berkeley Books, and in the United Kingdom and Europe by Airlift Book Company.

Cover illustration and design by Kathy Warinner
Interior design by Poulson Gluck Design

Telephone numbers, addresses and Website URLs are correct at the time of going to press and may be subject to subsequent alteration.

ISBN 1-58008-162-2

First printing, 2000
Printed in Canada

1 2 3 4 5 6 7 8 9 10 — 04 03 02 01 00

Contents

Preface

This journal is designed to be a flexible planning tool, resource, and memory book all in one. Use any of its extra features to plan and record your journey, or just write and sketch your way through the blank pages, taking inspiration from the words of other food-loving travelers.

The front part of the book allows you to gather some important trip information. Record vital personal data, notes on your destinations and itinerary, and your friends' and family members' addresses before you go. As you travel, take note of traveler's checks cashed and bank withdrawals made; photos taken; memorable meals eaten; and superlative wines tasted.

The blank journal pages are the heart of the book, and they're yours to fill. To help you find specific memories later, fill in the Journal Table of Contents on pages 44 and 45.

Following the journal pages and scattered throughout are inspirational quotes and practical tips, resources, and other features. So travel wisely and eat well—bon voyage and bon appétit!

Personal Data

Name . . . .

Address . . . .

. . . .

Telephone . . . .

Overseas address . . . .

. . . .

Overseas telephone . . . .

In case of emergency, please contact . . . .

. . . .

. . . .

. . . .

. . . .

Blood type . . . .

Special medical information . . . .

. . . .

Doctor's phone/fax numbers . . . .

. . . .

Religion . . . .

Passport number . . . .

Air/rail ticket numbers . . . .

. . . .

. . . .

For lost or stolen traveler's checks, call . . . .

For lost or stolen credit cards, call . . . .

For lost or stolen debit card, call . . . .

What to Pack

On a long journey even a straw weighs heavy.

—SPANISH PROVERB

To carry on the plane:

- ❏ airsickness and headache remedies
- ❏ cash, including enough local currency for taxi or bus fare
- ❏ change of clothes, shoes, underwear
- ❏ contact lens case and solution
- ❏ credit and debit cards and long-distance calling card
- ❏ customs papers and receipts
- ❏ driver's license
- ❏ earplugs
- ❏ eyeshade
- ❏ itinerary
- ❏ journal
- ❏ lip balm and makeup
- ❏ passport and visas
- ❏ pen
- ❏ portable CD or tape player (and music)
- ❏ reading material (including guide books)
- ❏ snacks and drinking water
- ❏ tickets
- ❏ toothbrush and toothpaste
- ❏ traveler's checks (in a money belt)
- ❏ travel pillow
- ❏ umbrella

In your other luggage:

- ❏ adapters/converters
- ❏ alarm clock/watch
- ❏ bandanna
- ❏ camera/batteries/film
- ❏ glasses/contacts (spare, plus prescription)
- ❏ hanger (inflatable)
- ❏ maps
- ❏ medications (Keep prescription medications in their original containers and carry written prescriptions.)
- ❏ passport photocopy
- ❏ safety pins/sewing kit
- ❏ string bag
- ❏ sunglasses
- ❏ Swiss army knife
- ❏ toiletries
- ❏ travel iron
- ❏ walking shoes

_____

_____

_____

_____

_____

_____

_____

Country Notes

Country _____

International access code/country code*_____

Currency/exchange rate** _____

Embassy/consulates*** _____

_____

Other _____

_____

Country _____

International access code/country code*_____

Currency/exchange rate** _____

Embassy/consulates*** _____

_____

Other _____

_____

Country _____

International access code/country code*_____

Currency/exchange rate** _____

Embassy/consulates*** _____

_____

Other _____

_____

Country _____

International access code/country code*_____

Currency/exchange rate** _____

Embassy/consulates*** _____

_____

Other _____

_____

Country _____

International access code/country code*_____

Currency/exchange rate** _____

Embassy/consulates*** _____

_____

Other _____

_____

*Find telephone international dialing codes and country codes in your travel guide book.

**Look up recent exchange rates in your local newspaper or online before you depart.

***Pick up consulate/embassy contact information, travel warnings, and bulletins for your destination country in your passport office, or contact your government directly:

> U.S. State Department Office
> of Overseas Citizens Services
>   202-647-5225
>   www.travel.state.gov

> Canadian Department of Foreign Affairs
> and International Trade
>   800-267-6788 or 613-944-6788
>   www.dfait-maeci.gc.ca/travel/menu-e.asp

Itinerary

A journey is like marriage.
The certain way to be wrong is to think you control it.

—JOHN STEINBECK

Destination_____

Departure/arrival dates and times_____

Accommodations _____

_____

Restaurants/markets/foods to sample _____

_____

_____

_____

_____

Destination_____

Departure/arrival dates and times_____

Accommodations _____

_____

Restaurants/markets/foods to sample _____

_____

_____

_____

_____

Destination_____

Departure/arrival dates and times_____

Accommodations _____

_____

Restaurants/markets/foods to sample _____

_____

_____

_____

_____

Destination_____

Departure/arrival dates and times_____

Accommodations _____

_____

Restaurants/markets/foods to sample _____

_____

_____

_____

_____

Destination_____

Departure/arrival dates and times_____

Accommodations _____

_____

Restaurants/markets/foods to sample _____

_____

_____

_____

_____

Destination_____

Departure/arrival dates and times_____

Accommodations _____

_____

Restaurants/markets/foods to sample _____

_____

_____

_____

_____

Destination_____

Departure/arrival dates and times_____

Accommodations _____

_____

Restaurants/markets/foods to sample _____

_____

_____

_____

_____

Destination_____

Departure/arrival dates and times_____

Accommodations _____

_____

Restaurants/markets/foods to sample _____

_____

_____

_____

_____

Addresses

NAME _____

    TELEPHONE _____

    ADDRESS _____

    E-MAIL _____

NAME _____

    TELEPHONE _____

    ADDRESS _____

    E-MAIL _____

NAME _____

    TELEPHONE _____

    ADDRESS _____

    E-MAIL _____

NAME _____

    TELEPHONE _____

    ADDRESS _____

    E-MAIL _____

NAME _____

    TELEPHONE _____

    ADDRESS _____

    E-MAIL _____

NAME _____

    TELEPHONE _____

    ADDRESS _____

    E-MAIL _____

NAME _____

    TELEPHONE _____

    ADDRESS _____

    E-MAIL _____

Addresses

NAME _____

    TELEPHONE _____

    ADDRESS _____

    E-MAIL _____

NAME _____

    TELEPHONE _____

    ADDRESS _____

    E-MAIL _____

NAME _____

    TELEPHONE _____

    ADDRESS _____

    E-MAIL _____

NAME _____

    TELEPHONE _____

    ADDRESS _____

    E-MAIL _____

NAME _____

    TELEPHONE _____

    ADDRESS _____

    E-MAIL _____

NAME _____

    TELEPHONE _____

    ADDRESS _____

    E-MAIL _____

NAME _____

    TELEPHONE _____

    ADDRESS _____

    E-MAIL _____

Record of Traveler's Checks, Credit Card Advances, and Debit Card Withdrawals

Check Number / Credit / Debit	Amount	Date & Place Cashed / Withdrawn	Exchange Rate

Record of Traveler's Checks, Credit Card Advances, and Debit Card Withdrawals

Check Number / Credit / Debit	Amount	Date & Place Cashed / Withdrawn	Exchange Rate

Record of Expenses

Keeping a record of expenses will help with budgeting as you travel and with customs when you get home. For more on shopping and shipping, see page 139.

Item	Amount

Item	Amount

Record of Photos

Roll #	Dates	Locations

Memorable Meals

Did you have a dish you loved in a restaurant or someone's home? Ask for the recipe! Write it down either below or on another journal page.

Date _October 1, 2004_

City _Québec_

Restaurant/Cook _Café de la Paix_

Guests _Mom, Hugh & me_

Dishes _____

Wines _Fabulous St Emilion_

Notes _Had a terrific Guinea Fowl with Calvados Sauce and caramelized apples. Vegs on the side plate — French style. Lovely baby greens in vinaigrette to start. Finished a fruit salad with Amaretto._

Fabulous meal.

Date_____

City _____

Restaurant/Cook _____

Guests _____

_____

_____

Dishes _____

_____

_____

_____

_____

Wines _____

_____

_____

Notes_____

_____

_____

_____

_____

_____

_____

_____

_____

_____

_____

_____

Date_____

City _____

Restaurant/Cook _____

Guests _____

_____

_____

Dishes _____

_____

_____

_____

_____

Wines _____

_____

_____

Notes_____

_____

_____

_____

_____

_____

_____

_____

_____

_____

_____

_____

Date_____

City _____

Restaurant/Cook _____

Guests _____

_____

_____

Dishes _____

_____

_____

_____

_____

Wines _____

_____

_____

Notes_____

_____

_____

_____

_____

_____

_____

_____

_____

_____

_____

Date_____

City _____

Restaurant/Cook _____

Guests_____

_____

_____

Dishes_____

_____

_____

_____

_____

Wines _____

_____

_____

Notes_____

_____

_____

_____

_____

_____

_____

_____

_____

_____

_____

_____

Date_____

City _____

Restaurant/Cook _____

Guests _____

_____

_____

Dishes _____

_____

_____

_____

_____

Wines _____

_____

_____

Notes_____

_____

_____

_____

_____

_____

_____

_____

_____

_____

_____

_____

Date_____

City _____

Restaurant/Cook _____

Guests _____

_____

_____

Dishes _____

_____

_____

_____

_____

Wines _____

_____

_____

Notes_____

_____

_____

_____

_____

_____

_____

_____

_____

_____

_____

_____

Date_____

City_____

Restaurant/Cook _____

Guests_____

_____

_____

Dishes_____

_____

_____

_____

_____

Wines_____

_____

_____

Notes_____

_____

_____

_____

_____

_____

_____

_____

_____

_____

_____

Date_____

City _____

Restaurant/Cook _____

Guests _____

_____

_____

Dishes _____

_____

_____

_____

_____

Wines _____

_____

_____

Notes_____

_____

_____

_____

_____

_____

_____

_____

_____

_____

_____

Date_____

City _____

Restaurant/Cook _____

Guests _____

_____

_____

Dishes _____

_____

_____

_____

_____

Wines _____

_____

_____

Notes_____

_____

_____

_____

_____

_____

_____

_____

_____

_____

_____

Date_____

City_____

Restaurant/Cook_____

Guests_____

_____
_____

Dishes_____

_____

_____

_____

_____

Wines_____

_____

_____

Notes_____

_____

_____

_____

_____

_____

_____

_____

_____

_____

_____

Date_____

City _____

Restaurant/Cook _____

Guests_____

_____

_____

Dishes _____

_____

_____

_____

_____

Wines _____

_____

_____

Notes_____

_____

_____

_____

_____

_____

_____

_____

_____

_____

_____

_____

Date_____

City _____

Restaurant/Cook _____

Guests _____

_____

_____

Dishes _____

_____

_____

_____

_____

Wines _____

_____

_____

Notes_____

_____

_____

_____

_____

_____

_____

_____

_____

_____

_____

Date_____

City _____

Restaurant/Cook _____

Guests _____

_____

_____

Dishes _____

_____

_____

_____

_____

Wines _____

_____

_____

Notes_____

_____

_____

_____

_____

_____

_____

_____

_____

_____

_____

Date_____

City _____

Restaurant/Cook _____

Guests _____

_____

_____

Dishes _____

_____

_____

_____

_____

Wines _____

_____

_____

Notes_____

_____

_____

_____

_____

_____

_____

_____

_____

_____

_____

Date_____

City _____

Restaurant/Cook _____

Guests _____

_____

_____

Dishes _____

_____

_____

_____

_____

Wines _____

_____

_____

Notes_____

_____

_____

_____

_____

_____

_____

_____

_____

_____

_____

_____

Date_____

City _____

Restaurant/Cook _____

Guests _____

_____

_____

Dishes _____

_____

_____

_____

_____

Wines _____

_____

_____

Notes_____

_____

_____

_____

_____

_____

_____

_____

_____

_____

_____

Date_____

City _____

Restaurant/Cook _____

Guests_____

_____

_____

Dishes_____

_____

_____

_____

_____

Wines_____

_____

_____

Notes_____

_____

_____

_____

_____

_____

_____

_____

_____

_____

_____

_____

Date_____

City _____

Restaurant/Cook _____

Guests_____

_____

_____

Dishes _____

_____

_____

_____

_____

_____

Wines _____

_____

_____

Notes_____

_____

_____

_____

_____

_____

_____

_____

_____

_____

_____

_____

_____

Date _____

City _____

Restaurant/Cook _____

Guests _____

_____

_____

Dishes _____

_____

_____

_____

_____

Wines _____

_____

_____

Notes _____

_____

_____

_____

_____

_____

_____

_____

_____

_____

_____

_____

Wine Journal

I only drink champagne when I'm happy, and when I'm sad. Sometimes I drink it when I'm alone. When I have company, I consider it obligatory. I trifle with it if I am not hungry and drink it when I am. Otherwise I never touch it—unless I'm thirsty.

—LILY BOLLINGER

Name of wine (varietal) _____

Vintage _____

Wine maker _____

Place of origin _____

Where purchased _____

Tasting notes _____

Name of wine (varietal) _____

Vintage _____

Wine maker _____

Place of origin _____

Where purchased _____

Tasting notes _____

Name of wine (varietal) _____

Vintage _____

Wine maker _____

Place of origin _____

Where purchased _____

Tasting notes _____

Name of wine (varietal) _____

Vintage _____

Wine maker _____

Place of origin _____

Where purchased _____

Tasting notes _____

Name of wine (varietal) _____

Vintage _____

Wine maker _____

Place of origin _____

Where purchased _____

Tasting notes _____

Name of wine (varietal) _____

Vintage _____

Wine maker _____

Place of origin _____

Where purchased _____

Tasting notes _____

Name of wine (varietal) _____

Vintage _____

Wine maker _____

Place of origin _____

Where purchased _____

Tasting notes _____

Name of wine (varietal) _____

Vintage _____

Wine maker _____

Place of origin _____

Where purchased _____

Tasting notes _____

Name of wine (varietal) _____

Vintage _____

Wine maker _____

Place of origin _____

Where purchased _____

Tasting notes _____

Name of wine (varietal) _____

Vintage _____

Wine maker _____

Place of origin _____

Where purchased _____

Tasting notes _____

Name of wine (varietal) _____

Vintage _____

Wine maker _____

Place of origin _____

Where purchased _____

Tasting notes _____

Journal Contents

I have more memories than if I had lived a thousand years.

— CHARLES BAUDELAIRE

PLACE/SUBJECT	PAGE

PLACE/SUBJECT	PAGE

DATE_____

PLACE_____

The discovery of a new dish does more for human happiness
than the discovery of a new star.

—ANTHELME BRILLAT-SAVARIN

DATE_____

PLACE_____

....

....

....

....

....

....

....

....

....

....

....

....

....

....

....

....

....

....

....

....

....

....

....

DATE _____

PLACE _____

DATE_____

PLACE_____

DATE_____

PLACE_____

....

....

....

....

....

....

....

No man can be a patriot on an empty stomach.

—WILLIAM COWPER

....

....

....

....

....

....

....

....

....

....

....

....

....

DATE_____

PLACE_____

. . . .

. . . .

. . . .

. . . .

. . . .

. . . .

. . . .

. . . .

. . . .

. . . .

. . . .

. . . .

. . . .

. . . .

. . . .

. . . .

. . . .

. . . .

. . . .

. . . .

. . . .

. . . .

. . . .

DATE_____

PLACE_____

I mind my belly very studiously, and very carefully;
for I look upon it, that he who does not mind his belly
will hardly mind anything else.

—SAMUEL JOHNSON

DATE _____

PLACE _____

DATE_____

PLACE_____

DATE _____

PLACE _____

Date_____

Place_____

. . . .

. . . .

. . . .

. . . .

. . . .

. . . .

. . . .

No man is lonely eating spaghetti; it requires so much attention.

—CHRISTOPHER DARLINGTON MORLEY

. . . .

. . . .

. . . .

. . . .

. . . .

. . . .

. . . .

. . . .

. . . .

. . . .

. . . .

DATE_____

PLACE_____

. . . .

. . . .

. . . .

. . . .

. . . .

. . . .

. . . .

. . . .

. . . .

. . . .

. . . .

. . . .

. . . .

. . . .

. . . .

. . . .

. . . .

. . . .

. . . .

. . . .

. . . .

. . . .

. . . .

. . . .

63

> *One cannot think well, love well, sleep well,*
> *if one has not dined well.*
>
> —VIRGINIA WOOLF

DATE_____

PLACE_____

. . . .
. . . .
. . . .
. . . .
. . . .
. . . .
. . . .
. . . .
. . . .
. . . .
. . . .
. . . .
. . . .
. . . .
. . . .
. . . .
. . . .
. . . .
. . . .
. . . .
. . . .

DATE_____

PLACE_____

. . . .
. . . .
. . . .
. . . .
. . . .
. . . .
. . . .
. . . .
. . . .
. . . .
. . . .
. . . .
. . . .
. . . .
. . . .
. . . .
. . . .
. . . .
. . . .
. . . .
. . . .
. . . .
. . . .
. . . .

DATE _____

PLACE _____

. . . .

. . . .

. . . .

. . . .

. . . .

. . . .

. . . .

He was a very valiant man who first adventured
on eating of oysters.

—JAMES I OF ENGLAND

. . . .

. . . .

. . . .

. . . .

. . . .

. . . .

. . . .

. . . .

. . . .

. . . .

DATE_____

PLACE_____

DATE_____

PLACE_____

. . . .
. . . .
. . . .
. . . .
. . . .
. . . .
. . . .
. . . .
. . . .
. . . .
. . . .
. . . .
. . . .
. . . .
. . . .
. . . .
. . . .
. . . .
. . . .
. . . .
. . . .
. . . .
. . . .
. . . .
. . . .
. . . .
. . . .

We may live without poetry, music and art;
We may live without conscience, and live without heart;
We may live without friends; we may live without books;
But civilized man cannot live without cooks.

—OWEN MEREDITH

DATE_____

PLACE_____

DATE_____

PLACE_____

DATE_____

PLACE_____

DATE_____

PLACE_____

DATE_____

PLACE_____

. . . .
. . . .
. . . .
. . . .
. . . .
. . . .
. . . .

How can you govern a country which has 246 varieties of cheese?

—CHARLES DEGAULLE

. . . .
. . . .
. . . .
. . . .
. . . .
. . . .
. . . .
. . . .
. . . .
. . . .
. . . .

DATE_____

PLACE_____

DATE_____

PLACE_____

There is no sincerer love than the love of food.

—GEORGE BERNARD SHAW

DATE _____

PLACE _____

....
....
....
....
....
....
....
....
....
....
....
....
....
....
....
....
....
....
....
....
....
....
....
....
....
....

. . . .
. . . .
. . . .
. . . .
. . . .
. . . .
. . . .
. . . .
. . . .
. . . .
. . . .
. . . .
. . . .
. . . .
. . . .
. . . .
. . . .
. . . .
. . . .
. . . .
. . . .
. . . .
. . . .

DATE _____

PLACE _____

....
....
....
....
....
....
....
....
....
....
....
....
....
....
....
....
....
....
....
....
....
....
....
....
....
....

DATE_____

PLACE_____

. . . .

. . . .

. . . .

. . . .

. . . .

. . . .

. . . .

A nickel will get you on the subway, but garlic will get you a seat.

—OLD NEW YORK PROVERB

. . . .

. . . .

. . . .

. . . .

. . . .

. . . .

. . . .

. . . .

. . . .

. . . .

. . . .

DATE _____

PLACE _____

. . . .

. . . .

. . . .

. . . .

. . . .

. . . .

. . . .

. . . .

. . . .

. . . .

. . . .

. . . .

. . . .

. . . .

. . . .

. . . .

. . . .

. . . .

. . . .

. . . .

. . . .

. . . .

. . . .

DATE_____

PLACE_____

. . . .

. . . .

. . . .

. . . .

. . . .

. . . .

. . . .

. . . .

. . . .

. . . .

. . . .

. . . .

. . . .

. . . .

. . . .

. . . .

. . . .

. . . .

. . . .

. . . .

. . . .

. . . .

After a few months' acquaintance with European "coffee," one's mind weakens, and his faith with it, and he begins to wonder if the rich beverage of home, with its clotted layer of yellow cream on top of it, is not a mere dream after all, and a thing which never existed.

—MARK TWAIN

DATE_____

PLACE_____

DATE_____

PLACE_____

DATE_____

PLACE_____

DATE_____

PLACE_____

DATE_____

PLACE_____

. . . .

. . . .

. . . .

. . . .

. . . .

. . . .

. . . .

We are a plain quiet folk and have no use for adventures.
Nasty disturbing uncomfortable things! Make you late for dinner!
I can't think what anybody sees in them!

—J. R. R. TOLKIEN

. . . .

. . . .

. . . .

. . . .

. . . .

. . . .

. . . .

. . . .

. . . .

DATE_____

PLACE_____

DATE_____

PLACE_____

....
....
....
....
....
....
....
....
....
....
....
....
....
....
....
....
....
....
....
....
....
....
....
....

Every journey has a chance to become a forced march,
commanded by the primacy of next meal and next bed.

—JOHN KRICH

DATE_____

PLACE_____

DATE_____

PLACE_____

DATE_____

PLACE_____

....

....

....

....

....

....

....

....

....

....

....

....

....

....

....

....

....

....

....

....

....

....

....

....

....

DATE_____

PLACE_____

....
....
....
....
....
....
....

The first condition of understanding
a foreign country is to smell it.

—RUDYARD KIPLING

....
....
....
....
....
....
....
....
....
....
....
....

DATE_____

PLACE_____

. . . .
. . . .
. . . .
. . . .
. . . .
. . . .
. . . .
. . . .
. . . .
. . . .
. . . .
. . . .
. . . .
. . . .
. . . .
. . . .
. . . .
. . . .
. . . .
. . . .
. . . .
. . . .
. . . .

DATE _____

PLACE _____

. . . .

. . . .

. . . .

. . . .

. . . .

. . . .

. . . .

. . . .

. . . .

. . . .

. . . .

. . . .

. . . .

. . . .

. . . .

. . . .

. . . .

. . . .

. . . .

. . . .

. . . .

. . . .

> *There's no sauce in the world like hunger.*
>
> —MIGUEL DE CERVANTES

DATE_____

PLACE_____

DATE_____

PLACE_____

DATE_____

PLACE_____

DATE_____

PLACE_____

DATE_____

PLACE_____

. . . .

. . . .

. . . .

. . . .

. . . .

. . . .

. . . .

No pudding, and no fun.

—QUEEN VICTORIA (UPON A DREADFUL INN IN SCOTLAND)

. . . .

. . . .

. . . .

. . . .

. . . .

. . . .

. . . .

. . . .

. . . .

. . . .

. . . .

DATE _____

PLACE _____

DATE_____

PLACE_____

. . . .

. . . .

. . . .

. . . .

. . . .

. . . .

. . . .

. . . .

. . . .

. . . .

. . . .

. . . .

. . . .

. . . .

. . . .

. . . .

. . . .

. . . .

. . . .

. . . .

. . . .

. . . .

. . . .

. . . .

If you come to a fork in the road, take it.

—YOGI BERRA

DATE_____

PLACE_____

DATE_____

PLACE_____

DATE_____

PLACE_____

DATE_____

PLACE_____

DATE_____

PLACE_____

. . . .

. . . .

. . . .

. . . .

. . . .

. . . .

. . . .

*If you reject the food, ignore the customs, fear the religion
and avoid the people, you might better stay at home.*

—JAMES A. MICHENER

. . . .

. . . .

. . . .

. . . .

. . . .

. . . .

. . . .

. . . .

. . . .

. . . .

. . . .

DATE_____

PLACE_____

DATE_____

PLACE_____

This was the moment I longed for every day.
Settling at a heavy inn-table, thawing and tingling,
with wine, bread, and cheese handy and my papers, books
and diary all laid out; writing up the day's doings.

—PATRICK LEIGH FERMOR

. . . .

. . . .

. . . .

. . . .

. . . .

. . . .

. . . .

. . . .

. . . .

. . . .

. . . .

. . . .

. . . .

. . . .

. . . .

. . . .

DATE_____

PLACE_____

. . . .

. . . .

. . . .

. . . .

. . . .

. . . .

. . . .

. . . .

. . . .

. . . .

. . . .

. . . .

. . . .

. . . .

. . . .

. . . .

. . . .

. . . .

. . . .

. . . .

. . . .

. . . .

. . . .

. . . .

DATE_____

PLACE_____

DATE_____

PLACE_____

DATE_____

PLACE_____

There are only three things which make life worth living:
to be writing a tolerably good book, to be in a dinner party
of six, and to be travelling south with someone
whom your conscience permits you to love.

— CYRIL CONNOLLY

DATE_____

PLACE_____

The autumn leaves are falling like rain;
Although my neighbors are all barbarians,
And you, you are a thousand miles away,
There are always two cups at my table.

—T'ANG DYNASTY VERSE

DATE_____

PLACE_____

The Wired Foodie

Various travel and food Websites can help you plan your trip and educate yourself about the cuisine (the Resources section of this book, pages 155–160, lists several good sites). With a little foresight, you can also use the Internet to guide you while you're on the road.

Make use of "Internet cafés," which have sprung up all over the world. Some of these establishments serve food, but most are just places where anyone can dial in to the Internet for a fee. Learn more about using them (and find many listings) online or in the book *Cybercafes* (see Resources section). Write some cybercafe addresses for your destination below.

Before you go, take a few minutes to capture the URLs of your favorite food and travel Websites. Write them in the space below (or print them out and tape them here) — or even add them to your personal Webpage as links, if you know how. Some good site addresses to take with you include:

- A currency calculator, such as the one on www.bloomberg.com

- An international restaurant guide, such as www.fodors.com

- A language translator, such as www.babylon.com

- Your favorite online guidebook, such as www.lonelyplanet.com

- The U.S. State Department Website (useful even for nationals of other countries), at www.state.gov

_____

_____

_____

_____

_____

Culinary Vacations

Culinary tours offer a hands-on introduction to the cuisine of a region or of an individual chef. These package vacations often combine cooking classes and educational excursions to local markets, farms, and restaurants with pleasant lodgings and company. At their best, they're a vivid immersion in the best a cuisine has to offer. So how do you find the best?

Start by thinking about where you want to **go**—Italy? Provence? New Orleans? How much do you want to **spend**? Do you want to relax and be pampered, or do you want to really add to your culinary skills and knowledge?

Now cast out your net for information. Contact specialty travel agents, both on and off-line, for **brochures.** Sift through magazines and newsletters, such as *Saveur* and *The Educated Traveler.* Consult a guide to cooking schools, such as the *Shaw Guide.* Can your friends provide any recommendations? Does your favorite chef or cookbook author run a cooking school? Once you've located a handful of programs that look appealing, investigate each further:

- What are the **classes** like? Are they hands-on lessons, demonstration, or a mix? Will you learn the why as well as the how of the cuisine? Are they appropriate to your skill level? How many students per class?

- Are the cooking and lodging **facilities** good? Will each student have his or her own station and equipment? Is it modern? Are there private rooms?

- Who is the **instructor**? What is his or her training and background? Will there be a language barrier between you? Try to get copies of some recipes, and talk to the instructor to get a feel for his or her teaching style and approach to the cuisine.

- What's **included** in the price? Are all meals, lodging, transportation, and excursions included, or will some of these cost extra? Where will you eat each day? How much free time is there? What excursions and tours are planned, and do they sound appealing to you?

- Request the names of recent participants and contact them to ask if they'd **recommend** the program, and why or why not.

Wine Tours

*Once, in the wilds of Afghanistan, I lost my corkscrew, and
we were forced to live on nothing but food and water for days.*

—W. C. FIELDS

A wine tour can be an unbeatable way of deepening your knowledge of a wine-producing region — and enriching your cellar.
Wine tourism centers around the great wine producing
regions—Napa Valley, California; Adelaide, South Australia;
provincial France; and so on. Winemakers from Hungary to
New England are also doing interesting things (though they
may not be as well served by guided tours).

Find wineries and wine tours before you go by contacting a specialized travel agent, or hop on the Internet to find tourist
boards in the great wine-producing regions. Before you book
one, ask some questions:

• What are your guide's qualifications and experience?

• What's included in the price? (meals? lodgings? lectures?
tastings?)

• Is transportation provided? (It's best not to have to drive
between tastings.)

• Will you be able to purchase wines and ship them home
directly?

• Will you be able to meet the winemakers themselves, or only
tasting room staff?

• Will your visit happen during a significant time in the winery
(the harvest; the bottling of the new Beaujolais)?

If you choose to visit any wineries without a guide, call ahead to
see if each has open hours when you can visit. Don't just drop
in—winemakers are busy folks.

Global Etiquette

Table manners and body language demonstrate your respect for members of other cultures. Customs vary widely, so try to learn the rudiments of good behavior before you visit. In a pinch, observe your native host or companions and follow their lead; in a restaurant, ask the waiter what is correct. Here are just a few tidbits of global etiquette:

In India, Muslim countries, and other societies where one eats with one's hands, eat only with your right hand; the left is usually considered unclean.

In Austria, it's impolite to begin eating before others in your party.

You may offer to pick up the tab if invited to a restaurant in Taiwan, but you'll probably be refused. Splitting the bill is boorish.

Thrifty Belgians expect guests to finish their meals, not waste food.

Bulgarians and Hungarians leave their napkins on the table during a meal, not in their laps.

In Colombia, don't serve yourself food before offering it to others first, and don't eat on the street.

Czechs remove their shoes upon entering a host's home and leave them in the entryway, as do Thais.

In Australia and Britain, the word "stuffed" has a sexual, not a gastronomical, connotation.

In Europe, the fork stays in the left hand, the knife in the right. Cut your food, then convey the bite to your mouth without switching the fork to your right hand (a North American custom).

Don't leave your chopsticks upright in a bowl of food.

In Ethiopia, if someone offers to feed you by hand, it's considered a great honor. Accept it.

In Europe and Asia, ask for the bill in a restaurant (either with words or a writing gesture); they won't bring it automatically when you seem to be done.

In France (and in Western-style restaurants everywhere), the position of your silverware on your plate sends signals to the waiter:

- Knife and fork crossed on plate, tines down: "I'm not done, just pausing a minute."

- Knife and fork parallel to each other, diagonally across the plate from bottom right, tines down: "I'm done; you can take this plate away."

- Knife and fork parallel to each other across the top of the plate, tines down: "May I have some more of this delicious food, please?"

The service charge is usually included in the bill in most European countries, but a small (5 percent) gratuity may be added to recognize good service. In Iceland, however, tipping is considered an insult.

In Nicaragua, praise the food you're served in someone's home; in India, do not mention it.

Refusing an invitation in Pakistan is very rude, but staring at people you don't know is not.

When a Pole flicks his neck with his finger, he's inviting you to have a drink of vodka with him.

Be prepared: Russian vodka bottles, once opened, are meant to be emptied.

In Korea, don't eat with your fingers, but do slurp the noodles.

Don't point your finger at people in El Salvador or Malaysia.

Meals in Italy can last up to four hours. It's considered impolite to put your hands in your lap or to stretch at the table.

Silences are considered part of table conversation in Japan— don't rush to fill them.

In Fiji and in Ireland, refusing a proferred drink is insulting.

In France, most fruit is peeled with a knife and eaten with a fork (grapes are an exception).

Never touch anyone's hand in Indonesia—the hand is thought to be where the spirit resides.

In Kuwait, you must eat to bursting to show your appreciation of the meal.

_____

_____

_____

_____

_____

_____

_____

_____

_____

_____

_____

_____

_____

Staying Healthy

1. *Turn all care out of your head
   as soon as you mount the chaise.*

2. *Do not think about frugality:
   your health is worth more than it can cost.*

3. *Do not continue any day's journey to fatigue.*

4. *Take now and then a day's rest.*

5. *Get a smart seasickness if you can.*

6. *Cast away all anxiety, and keep your mind easy.*

*This last direction is the principal; with an unquiet mind
neither exercise, nor diet, nor physic can be of much use.*

—SAMUEL JOHNSON (ADVICE TO TRAVELERS)

On the plane. Wear loose clothing. Get up and walk around every half-hour. Drink plenty of water, and minimal alcohol or caffeinated drinks (these dehydrate your body). Take healthy snacks with you on the plane, such as fruit, unsalted nuts, or trail mix. Order a vegetarian or kosher meal in advance (these are often healthier options than regular airplane meals).

In the tropics and elsewhere. Going someplace where sanitation is poor? If you suspect the water, don't brush your teeth with it, put ice in your drinks, or eat raw fruits or vegetables that can't be peeled. Don't accept bottled water with a broken seal (the bottle may have been refilled with tap water).

Purify your water by boiling it (get a full, rolling boil going) or by using iodine tablets or a portable water filter. (Warning: too much iodine can be toxic, so don't rely on it alone. It also tastes bad—bring some powdered drink mix to mask the taste.)

Avoid meat and dairy foods — they, after water, are most often tainted. Make sure your cooked food is hot, and hasn't been sitting around a while. Finally, take a peek in restaurants at who's making and serving your food. If the staff look dirty, go elsewhere. (This applies anywhere you travel.)

In general. Any travel—even between highly industrialized countries—stresses your system. You will adapt to new time zones and diet changes — just rest and be careful what you eat and drink for the first few days. Drink lots of water, especially if in hot weather. Try to keep up your dietary fiber intake, as well, bringing supplements with you if desired.

To research immunizations and health alerts for your destination countries, contact the U.S. Centers for Disease Control at www.cdc.gov/travel/travel.html or by calling 877-394-8747. For a list of English-speaking physicians abroad, contact the International Association for Medical Assistance to Travelers (IAMAT) at 716-754-4883.

Shopping and Shipping

It is only the unexpected
that ever makes a customs officer think.

—FREYA STARK

Keep your receipts and use the space provided on page 18 to record your purchases. You'll need all this information to sort out your customs declaration.

BARGAIN HUNTING

A Sufi saying declares that a wise merchant knows what a thing is worth and what it costs (often not the same thing), and also what he is willing to pay for it. The same could be said of a wise shopper. If you go abroad looking for bargains:

- Do your **research** before you go. What goods make your destination famous, and what would they cost you at home? Sometimes a fine Turkish carpet will cost less in Manhattan than in Ankara.

- Take a **calculator** to figure currency exchange while you're shopping. Your currency confusion may make a deal sound better than it is.

- If you're the organized sort, make a **list** of the items you'd like to find or the people you're buying gifts for. This can help you avoid ill-considered impulse purchases, just as it does at home.

- Consider **duty-free** purchases carefully. Duty-free shops in airports may be good sources for highly taxed luxury items such as perfumes and jewelry. However, your selection is limited to the items these shops stock; the merchants pay high rents and may not pass sizable savings on to you; and, if you buy over your customs limit, you may find yourself paying duties on your purchases after all.

- Make sure you understand a store's **return and exchange** policies; they may be less generous than those you're used to.

- **Negotiate.** If a price seems too high to you, suggest a lower one. In some cultures (including many Middle Eastern countries), it's expected, and the merchant will start by naming a price that's several times higher than he's willing to sell it for.

- Consider using a **guide** or tout to show you around a bazaar or souk. Touts can show you the way, but be aware they will likely steer you to merchants who give them a cut. Fix your guide's fee in advance. If you don't use a guide, tell this to the merchants you buy from, so they're not figuring in a commission as they bargain with you.

- If you don't feel comfortable with how your purchase is going, simply **walk away.**

SHIPPING

Rather than carrying your purchases around as additions to your luggage:

- See if the shopkeeper can package and ship your purchase directly home for you. Make sure to keep the receipts and copies of the shipping documents for customs.

- If you make small purchases under your customs limit, consider mailing them home to yourself. Mark on the outside of the package "goods for personal use," so the package will clear customs.

- If you've made substantial and bulky purchases, you may need to engage a freight forwarder, who can ship your goods and guide them through customs. If you think you'll need one, try to locate one before you depart.

VAT

Several countries in Europe allow travelers to avoid paying the usually-hefty value-added tax (VAT) on certain goods. Policies vary, but you can usually either waive VAT if you ship your purchase home directly from the shop, or receive a refund in the mail after you return home (keep your receipts!). Consult an up-to-date travel guide book for a country's VAT policies.

CUSTOMS

Learn your own country's rules before you travel, and keep receipts for all purchases made abroad. For free customs information:

- In the U.S.A., send a stamped, self-addressed envelope to "Know Before You Go," Superintendent of Documents, Government Printing Office, Washington, D.C., 20402. Also available through many post offices or online at http://www.customs.ustreas.gov/

- In Canada, request a copy of Canada Customs and Revenue Agency's "I Declare/Je déclare" through your local customs office (look in the government pages of the phone book). Also available online at http://www.ccra-adrc.gc.ca/customs/individuals/menu-e.html

FORBIDDEN FRUITS

Items that will get you in legal trouble—either with your own government or that of the country of purchase—include:

- Wildlife souvenirs. Both live animals or skins and bones may be contraband. Only buy them if you're sure they're legal for both export from the country of purchase and import into your own.

- Antiques. Buy culturally important antiques only from an irreproachable dealer. Be sure you know what is permissible to export from a country, and keep your documents in order. If you buy a reproduction, get and keep written proof that that's what it is.

- Food and agricultural products. As an individual traveler you won't be able to bring foodstuffs home with you. Perhaps you'd prefer to let the memory nourish you, like Proust's madeleine. But if you find a brand of canned tomato or a variety of cheese you love and don't want to keep living without, why not contact the maker and ask if anyone imports it into your home country?

Find the Best Food in Restaurants

In a restaurant, choose a table near a waiter.

—JEWISH PROVERB

Before you go. If you want one or more world-class meals, do your research before you go. Learn some menu terms and something about the region's cuisine, and find a good restaurant guide (or a guide book with a good restaurant section).

The Michelin Red Guides are the most highly regarded restaurant (and hotel) guides in Europe. If it has a Michelin star, you know it's good. Other good guides are Fodor's and Lonely Planet's food guide series. Online restaurant guides are plentiful, but vary in quality. Several are listed in the Resources section (pages 155 to 160).

Ask around. Get recommendations from people who have visited (or, better, lived in) your destination. But be aware that fellow visitors are usually tourists too—and that things may have changed since they haunted the trattoria they rhapsodize about.

Better still is to ask a cab driver, desk clerk, or other native where they like to eat. Try to get beyond recommendations for restaurants they think you'll like (that is, tourist restaurants) to discover the places they like to eat. Ask what restaurant they'd choose if they wanted to propose marriage.

When you're wandering the streets of a strange town in search of a restaurant, look for a place that's full but has no tourists. Those are good signs.

What to order? If a chef has a great reputation, ask your server what the specialties of the house are. Otherwise, stick with food that's been produced and prepared locally for years, and it's hard to go wrong.

- In Greece, seek out lamb dishes.

- In Italy, eat veal and fresh, simply prepared produce.

- In Germany, sample sausages and beer.

- In China, pork is king.

- In the Middle East, chicken tends to be delectable.

- In France, you can spend a long, happy life
  eating cheese and drinking wine.

- In Belgium, get thee to a chocolatier.

- In Spain, try ham.

- In Southeast Asia, duck dishes shine.

- London has the best Indian food in the world
  (including India).

- In the southern central U.S., barbecue is an art form.

- If you don't eat fish in Japan or Hawaii,
  you've missed the boat.

Find the Best Food al Fresco

Parisian housewives don't need cookbooks.
The butcher, poultryman, and fishmonger all willingly
dispense verbal recipes with each purchase.

—PATRICIA WELLS

Food sold by street vendors or in market stalls is often fresh, authentic, and unforgettable. It can be a gustatory highlight of your trip.

Small Markets. If you're planning a picnic, or if you just wonder what it's like to shop in a foreign town, head to the market square or farmer's market (ask at your hotel). In many countries, vegetables, fish, sausages, milk, fruits, baked goods, and so on are sold separately in small shops or market stalls. The best vendors tend to be very knowledgeable about their wares—in farmer's markets, the seller may also be the grower.

Food Festivals. Food festivals and agricultural fairs offer unique insights into a region's culture and cuisine. Festivals linked to religious holidays or to the harvest tend to incorporate craft shows, music, games, and agricultural exhibits.

Others, strictly attuned to food, focus on restaurant cooking (like Paris's Fête de la Cuisine, in May), or feature cooking demonstrations (like Bangkok's Thailand International Food Exhibition, also in May), or both (like Australia's Feast of Sydney, in late June).

To find food festivals, consult your travel agent or guide book, check out the searchable database at www.whatsgoingon.com, or just ask around when you get there (you'll be likelier to find them in summer or early fall).

Street Food. Near farmer's markets and at food festivals—and dotting streets in every city are carts, stalls, and open-air kitchens producing simple, cheap food. The dishes are usually local specialties, though sometimes immigrants to a country add their own native dishes to the mix (for instance, you can get great Greek gyros on the streets of Paris). Here are just a few examples of what to try:

Mexico: tamales (stuffed cornmeal bundles)
and chiles rellenos (stuffed peppers)

France: sweet crepes and savory galettes
(thin, filled cakes)

Benelux and the Netherlands:
fried potatoes and doughnuts

Great Britain: fish and chips
(with lots of vinegar and salt!)

Spain: tortilla (a potato omelet)

North Africa: tagines (slow-cooked clay pot dishes)

India: chappatis and masala dosai (fried breads)
and sweets

Indonesia: campur rice (rice with cooked vegetables
and meats) and saté (grilled, skewered chunks of meat)

East Asia: noodle dishes of all kinds

Italy: ice cream, grilled chestnuts,
and more regional treats than you can imagine

Street vendors often cluster near farmer's markets. Cooked street food is, on average, as safe as restaurant food. In ordering from a street vendor, follow food safety rules (page 137) and don't order or eat anything your instincts tell you not to.

Glossary of Food Terms

	ENGLISH	FRENCH
Meat, Poultry, and Fish	meat	la viande
	beef	la viande de boeuf
	steak	le bifteck
	rare	saignant
	medium	à point
	well-done	bien cuit
	roast beef	le rosbif
	lamb	l'agneau (masc.)
	ham	le jambon
	veal	le veau
	pork	le porc
	sausage	une saucisse
	chicken	le poulet
	duck	le canard
	goose	la oie
	turkey	le dindon
	fish	le poisson
	salmon	le saumon
	sole	la sole
	trout	la truite
Eggs and Dairy	egg	un oeuf
	milk	le lait
	cream	la crème
	cheese	le fromage
Vegetables and Fruits	rice	le riz
	vegetable	un légume
	artichoke	un artichaut
	asparagus	l'asperge (fem.)
	beans	les fèves (fem.)
	carrot	une carotte
	cucumbers	un concombre
	lettuce	la laitue

ITALIAN	SPANISH	GERMAN
la carne	la carne	das Fleisch
il manzo	la carne de res	das Rindfleisch
la bistecca	el bistec	das Beefsteak
al sangue	poco cocida/hecha	leicht angebraten
cottura media	en un término medio	mittelgebraten
ben cotta	bien cocida	gut durchgebraten
il manzo arrosto	el rosbif	der Rinderbraten
il agnello	el cordero	das Lamm
il prosciutto	el jamón	der Schinken
la carne di vitello	la ternera	der Kalbfleish
la carne di maiale	la carne de cerdo	das Schweinefleisch
una salsiccia	una salchicha	eine Wurst
il pollo	el pollo	das Huhn
l'anitra	el pato	die Ente
l'oca	el ganso	die Gans
il tacchino	el pavo	der Truthahn
il pesce	el pescado	der Fisch
lo salmone	el salmón	der Lachs
la sogliola	el lenguado	die Seezunge
la trota	la trucha	die Forelle
un uovo	un huevo	ein Ei
il latte	la leche	die Milch
la crema	la crema	die Sahne
il formaggio	el queso	der Käse
il riso	el arroz	das Reis
un vegetale	una verdura	das Gemüse
un carciofo	un alcacil (Sp.)/una alcachofa (Am.)	eine Artischocke
le asparagi	los espárragos	der Spargel
I fagioli	los frijoles	die Bohnen
una carota	una zanahoria	eine Karotte
un cetriolo	un pepino	eine Gurke
la lattuga	la lechuga	der Salat

ENGLISH	FRENCH
peas	les pois (masc.)
potato	une pomme de terre
spinach	les épinards (masc.)
tomato	une tomate
fruit	un fruit
apple	une pomme
banana	une banane
cherry	une cerise
grape	un raisin
lemon	un citron
orange	une orange
peach	une pêche
pear	une poire
strawberry	une fraise

Sweets

ENGLISH	FRENCH
dessert	le dessert
pastry	une pâtisserie
chocolate	le chocolat
ice cream	la glace

Drinks

ENGLISH	FRENCH
beer	la bière
wine	le vin
red wine	vin rouge
white wine	vin blanc
water (bottled)	l'eau (de source)
with ice	avec des glaçons
juice	le jus
coffee	le café
coffee with milk	café au lait
tea	le thé
herbal tea	thé d'herbe
straight	sec
with water	à l'eau
with soda	avec soda
sugar	le sucre

ITALIAN	SPANISH	GERMAN
I piselli	los guisantes Sp.)/ las arvejas (Am.)	die Erbsen
una patata	una patata (Sp.)/ un papa (Am.)	eine Kartoffel
I spinaci	las espinacas	der Spinat
un pomodoro	un tomate	eine Tomate
la frutta	una fruta	das Obst
una mela	una manzana	ein Apfel
una banana	un plátano	eine Banane
una ciliegia	una cereza	eine Kirsche
un acino	una uva	eine Weintraube
un limone	un limón	eine Zitrone
un'arancia	una naranja	eine Orange
una pesca	un melocotón/ un durazno	ein Pfirsich
una pera	una pera	eine Birne
una fragola	una fresa	eine Erdbeere
il dolce	el postre	der Nachtisch
una pasta	un pastel	ein Gebäck
il cioccolato	el chocolate	die Schokolade
il gelato	el helado	das Eis
la birra	la cerveza	das Bier
il vino	el vino	der Wein
vino rosso	vino tinto	der Rotwein
vino bianco	vino blanco	der Weißwein
l'acqua (pottabile)	agua (embotellada)	das Mineralwasser
con ghiaccio	con hielo	mit Eis
lo succo	el jugo	der Saft
il caffè	el café	der Kaffee
caffè latte	café con leche	Kaffee mit Milch
il tè	el té	der Tee
tè dell'erba	té de la hierba	Kräutertee
liscio	puro	nicht verdünnt
con acqua	con agua	mit Wasser
con soda	con soda	mit Seltserwasser
lo zucchero	el azúcar	der Zucker

	ENGLISH	FRENCH
Other Foods	sandwich	sandwich
	salad	la salade
	soup	la soupe
	bread	le pain
	butter	le beurre
	salt	le sel
	pepper	le poivre
Other Food-Related Terms and Phrases	cup	une tasse
	plate	une assiette
	glass	un verre
	napkin	une serviette
	fork	une fourchette
	spoon	une cuillère
	knife	une couteau
	vegetarian	végétarien
	diabetic	diabétique
	restaurant	un restaurant
	café	un café
	bar	une buvette
	breakfast	le petit-déjeuner
	lunch	le déjeuner
	dinner	le dîner
	to be thirsty	avoir soif
	to be hungry	avoir faim
	baked	cuit au four
	boiled	bouilli
	fried	frit
	roasted	rôti
	steamed	cuit
	hot	chaud
	cold	froid
	expensive	cher
	inexpensive	bon marché
	grocery store	l'épicerie (fem.)
	market	le marché

ITALIAN	SPANISH	GERMAN
un tramezzino	un sandwich	ein Sandwich
la insalata	la ensalada	der Salat
la minestra	la sopa	die Suppe
il pane	el pan	das Brot
il burro	la mantequilla	die Butter
lo sale	la sal	das Salz
il pepe	la pimienta	der Pfeffer
una tazza	una taza	eine Tasse
un piatto	un plato	eine Platte/ eine Scheibe
un bicchiere	un vaso	ein Glas
un tovagliolo	una servilleta	eine Serviette
una forchetta	un tenedor	ein Gabel
un cucchiaio	una cuchara	ein Löffel
un coltello	un cuchillo	ein Messer
vegetariano	vegetariano	Vegetarier
diabetico	diabético	Diabetiker
un ristorante	un restaurante	ein Restaurant
un caffè	un café	ein Café
un bar	un bar	eine Bar
la colazione	el desayuno	das Frühstück
il pranzo	el almuerzo	das Mittagessen
la cena	la cena	das Abendessen
aver sete	tener sed	Durst haben
aver fame	tener hambre	hungrig sein
cotto	cocido al horno	gebacken
bollito	hervido	gekocht
fritto	frito	gebraten
arrostito	asado	gerösten
cotto a vapore	cocido al vapor	gedämpft
caldo	caliente	heiß
freddo	frío	kalt
costoso	caro	teuer
poco costoso	barato	billig
la drogheria	la abacería/ la bodega (Am.)	das Lebensmittelgeschäft
il mercato	el mercado	der Markt

English	French
Where is the farmer's market in this town?	Où est le marché des fermiers de cette ville?
Do you have a favorite restaurant?	Avez-vous un restaurant préféré?
Where can I find the best food in town?	Où puis-je trouver la meilleure cuisine en ville?

	English	French
In a Restaurant	pardon me	pardonnez-moi
	please	s'il vous plaît
	thank you	merci
	a table for two	une table pour deux personnes
	at eight o'clock	à huit heures
	at 8:30 (8:15/8:45)	à huit heures trente (quinze/quarante-cinq)
	I would like…	Je voudrais…
	May I have…	Puis-j'avoir
	the menu	la carte
	the wine list	la carte des vins
	Is there a house specialty?	Y a-t-il une spécialité de la maison?
	Please recommend a wine.	Veuillez recommander un vin, s'il vous plaît.
	waiter/waitress	serveur/serveuse
	The bill, please.	L'addition, s'il vous plaît.
	Is service included?	Est-ce que le service est compris?
	There's a mistake.	Il y a une erreur.
	This is for you.	C'est pour vous.
	Keep the change	Gardez la change.

ITALIAN	SPANISH	GERMAN
Dove è il mercato dei coltivatori di questa città?	Dónde está el mercado de los granjeros en esta ciudad?	Wo ist der Markt der Landwirte in dieser Stadt?
Avete un ristorante favorito?	Usted tiene un restaurante preferido?	Haben Sie eine Lieblingsgaststätte?
Dove posso trovare la cucina migliore in città?	Dónde puedo encontrar la mejor cocina de la ciudad?	Wo kann ich das beste Kochen in der Stadt finden?
perdonarlo	perdóneme	enshuldigen Sie
prego	por favor	bitte
grazie	gracias	danke
Un tavolo per due.	Una mesa para dos personas.	ein Tisch für zwei Leute
ad otto in punto	a las ocho	um acht Uhr
ad otto e trenta (e quindici/e quarantacinque)	a las ocho y media (y quince/ cuarenta y cinco)	um acht Uhr dreißig (fünfzehn/ fünfundvierzig)
Vorrei...	Quisiera...	Ich möchte...
Potrei avere...	Puedo tener...	Ich bitte um...
il menu	la carta/el menú	die Speisekarte
la lista dei vini	la carta de vinos	die Weinkarte
È ci una specialità della casa?	Hay una especialidad de la casa?	Gibt es ein Spezialgebiet des Hauses?
Suggerire prego un vino.	Recomiende por favor un vino.	Empfehlen Sie bitte ein Wein.
cameriere/?	camarero/a	der Kellner/die Kellnerin
Il conto, per favore.	La cuenta, por favor.	Die Rechnung, bitte.
Il servizio è incluso?	Se incluye el servicio?	Wird der Service umfaßt?
C'e un errore.	Hay un error.	Es gibt einen Fehler.
Ciò è per voi.	Esto está para usted.	Dieses ist für Sie.
Tenga pure il resto.	Guarde el cambio.	Halten Sie der Wechsel.

Conversion Charts

WEIGHT

1 ounce = 28.3 grams
1 gram = .035 ounce
1 pound = .45 kilogram
1 kilogram = 2.2 pounds

LENGTH

1 inch = 2.54 centimeters
1 centimeter = .39 inches
1 foot = 30.48 centimeters
1 meter = 3.28 feet
1 mile = 1.61 kilometers
1 kilometer = .62 miles

VOLUME

1 fluid ounce = 30 milliliters
1 pint = .47 liter
1 liter = 1.06 quarts

TEMPERATURE

°F	−40	32	41	50	59	68	86	100	104
°C	−40	0	5	10	15	20	30	38	40

SIMPLE FORMULAS FOR CONVERTING TEMPERATURES:

$9/5 C + 32 = F$
$(F-32) 5/9 = C$

VOLTAGES AND PLUGS

There are two main voltage standards (110/120 and 220/240) and at least nine different plug configurations in the world. To discover if those of your destination differ from those of your home, consult your travel guide book, or type the words "voltage standard" or "electrical plug," plus the name of your destination, into an Internet search engine. If the standard of your destination varies from that of your home, try to buy converters or transformers before you depart. Look in travel specialty stores or electronics stores, or search online.

Resources

BOOKS FOR FURTHER READING

Adventures on the Wine Route
by Kermit Lynch (Noonday, 1990)
The travels of a great American wine importer.

Culinaria
Könemann's series of opulently photographed books
cover European, North American, and Caribbean cuisines
are encyclopedic and inspirational, and contain excellent
canonical recipes.

*Much Depends on Dinner: The Extraordinary History and Mythology,
Allure and Obsessions, Perils and Taboos, of an Ordinary Meal*
by Margaret Visser (Grove, 1999)
Visser unravels the cultural and geographical travels
of the nine ingredients of a simple meal.

The Oysters of Locmariaquer
by Eleanor Clark (Ecco Press, 1998)
Winner of the National Book Award in 1965, this brilliantly
evocative book of oystermen in Brittany is a classic.

South Wind Through the Kitchen: The Best of Elizabeth David
by Elizabeth David (North Point Press, 1998)
A collection of the choicest morsels from the great food writer
and high priestess of Mediterranean cooking.

Two Towns in Provence
by M. F. K. Fisher (Vintage, 1983)
A compilation of two of Fisher's unforgettable portraits
of French towns: Aix and Marseille.

Under the Tuscan Sun: At Home in Italy
by Frances Mayes (Broadway, 1998)
Frances Mayes lives the dream of many: she spends her
summers tending her own olive orchards at her villa in
Tuscany, then she writes books about it.

A Weakness for Almost Everything:
Notes on Life, Gastronomy, and Travel
by Aldo Buzzi (Steerforth, 1999)
Buzzi is a Milanese architect and eccentric who writes with
gusto of food, travel, and the good life in general.

Won Ton Lust
by John Krich (Kodansha, 1997)
The gonzo author samples some 350 Chinese restaurants
around the world, trying to find the best one.

A Year in Provence
by Peter Mayle (Vintage, 1991)
A charming, food-filled novel.

RESOURCES

Australian Wine Online
You love the stuff, here's where to learn all about it and those
who make it. www.winetitles.com.au/wineonline

Citysearch.com
Find reviewed restaurants in a number of North American and
European cities. www.citysearch.com

Margaret Cowan

Cowan offers in-depth reviews in her book *110 Cooking Vacations in Italy*. She also offers tours herself. Contact: Margaret Cowan Direct Ltd., Suite 310, 101-1184 Denman Street Vancouver, BC, Canada V6G 2M9; also www.italycookingschools.com/index

Cybercafes by cyberkath@traveltales.com (Ten Speed Press, 1999) A guidebook to cybercafés around the world, including hundreds of listings.

The Discerning Traveler

A much-lauded newsletter covering the eastern U.S. Contact: 504 West Mermaid Lane, Philadelphia, PA 19118 U.S.A.; also www.discerningtraveler.com

Do's and Taboo's Around the World and Gestures —
The Do's and Taboo's of Body Language Around the World
by Roger E. Axtell (John Wiley & Sons, 1993 and 1998)
Handy etiquette guides, aimed at business travelers. Available in the travel section of many bookstores.

The Educated Traveler

Bimonthly newsletter, directory of specialty tour operators. Contact: P.O Box 220822, Chantilly, VA 20153 U.S.A.; also www.educated-traveler.com

The Fat Guy's Big Apple Dining Guide

Steven Shaw's Website is a terrific independent source for restaurant reviews in New York (where he lives) and a few other places he's visited. It's a treasure chest of intelligent, opinionated commentary from a guy who really loves food.
www.shaw-review.com

Eat Your Way Across the U.S.A.

by Jane and Michael Stern (Broadway, 1999)
The Sterns have long been the road warriors of American regional cuisine, seeking out good authentic food. The subtitle, "500 Diners, Farmland Buffets, Lobster Shacks, Pie Palaces, and Other All-American Eateries," says it all.

Epicurious
This large and sleek gourmet site is the online home of *Bon Appétit* and *Gourmet* magazines. www.epicurious.com

The Fearless Shopper: How to Get the Best Deals on the Planet
by Kathy Borrus (Traveler's Tales, 1999)
Savvy tips and a region-by-region global shopping guide from a pro.

Fodors Restaurant Finder
This site covers the globe from Anchorage to Zurich. An excellent, up to date resource. http://www.fodors.com/ri.cgi

The Food Lover's Guide to Paris (4th edition)
by Patricia Wells (Workman, 1999)
There are plenty of gourmet guides to Paris, but Wells's knowledge and love of Paris and of food make this the essential one.

Interactive dining guides
These are several of the many Web-based restaurant guides that rely wholly or partially on user reviews (as opposed to professional reviewers):

> The Active Diner www.activediner.com
> CuisineNet www.cuisinenet.com
> Dine.com www.dine.com
> The Phantom Gourmet
>   www.townonline.com/arts/dining/phantom
> Restaurant Row www.restaurantrow.com
> The Sushi Guide (for restaurants outside of Japan)
>   www.sushi.infogate.de
> The Ultimate Restaurant Directory
>   www.orbweavers.com/ULTIMATE

The Kosher Restaurant Database
A good resource for any international traveler, this interactive dining guide lists restaurants, markets, and food shops from Argentina to Ukraine, has some refreshingly honest reviews, and tells when the information was last updated.
www.shamash.org/kosher

The Lonely Planet World Food Guides
This practical and inspirational series presents in depth information on various national cuisines—including Mexico, Thailand, Italy, and Spain—from home cooking to restaurants to regional wines and specialties. Includes maps, recipes, photographs, and glossaries.

The Non-Connoisseur's Menu Guide
by David D'Aprix (Living Language, 1999)
A pocket guide to restaurant dining in France, Italy, Spain, and Latin America. Copious glossaries (with pronunciation help).

Sally's Place
Reviews restaurants around the world (mostly North America at this writing), and has great columnists and interesting articles.
www.sallys-place.com/food

The Shaw Guide to Cooking Schools
The book and Website list hundreds of cooking vacations, as well as professional schools. Indexed by cuisine, location, and time frame. Contact: ShawGuides, Inc., P.O. Box 231295, New York, NY 10023 U.S.A.; also www.shawguides.com/cook

Thailand Tourism & Travel Directory Language Translator
This fantastic free Website translates basic words and phrases from dozens of world languages (Hindi! Galician!), including audio files so you can hear how the words sound.
www.thailand-travelsearch.com/thailand/language

Transitions Abroad magazine
Thoughtful articles on destinations and modes of travel from ecotourism to study abroad. Information about tour operators broken down by specialty and country. Contact: Transitions Abroad Publishing, P.O. Box 1300, Amherst, MA 01004 U.S.A.; also www.transitionsabroad.com

Travelroads.com
Find tour operators and request free brochures. Search by destination or activity. www.travelroads.com

The Vegetarian Resource Group
Nonprofit publishers of the magazine *Vegetarian Journal, Vegetarian Journal's Guide to Natural Food Restaurants in the U.S. and Canada,* and a Website that hosts a bulletin board for vegetarian and vegan travelers and an online resource guide. www.vrg.org

Wine Spectator
The magazine's Website makes all its past travel articles available in one place, provides a searchable database of resorts and hotels, and features occasional "on the road" postings from the magazine's globe-trotting, wine-tasting editors.
www.winespectator.com/Wine/Spectator/Travel

World Guide to Vegetarianism
Users contribute brief reviews of far-flung restaurants to this Website. www.veg.org/veg/Guide

_____

_____

_____

_____

_____

_____

_____

_____

_____

_____

_____

_____

_____